WITHOUT A FIGHT

J D Whitaker

CONTENTS

CHAPTER ONE:
THE WANT

Twelve AM on a Friday night, she sat on the couch and continued to swipe right on Tinder to find the next man to ruin her life. Appearing on a screen, there he was, by the name of Dumane. He had fresh chocolate skin, bulging fish eye balls and beautiful pearly white teeth. A message appeared in her inbox. "Hey beautiful". She smiled and replied within seconds. The fact that she had just got out of a five year relationship and might possibly still is vulnerable slipped her mind.

Although she knew it was stupid, the two agreed to meet in a Walmart parking lot around three in the afternoon. Natalia arrived first. She sat and patiently waited anticipating his arrival. She called him and asked how far away he was, since he was coming from another city. He stated he was getting ready to pull up. Butterflies started to fill her stomach while wetness started to fill her underpants. She pulled her visor down to check her teeth and face one last time for perfection. She let the visor back up and up pulled a grey Ferrari. Dumane stepped out of his car, approached Natalia, gave her a hug and said "you are very beautiful in person and I'm glad I met you".

Natalia smiled in disbelief that somebody tall, dark, and semi handsome was this polite. She continued while sitting on her car "tell me about yourself". Dumane smiled and explained that he owned a million dollar business, has a hous no kids, fought and beat cancer, played pro basketball overseas but got hurt and couldn't continue. Natalia started to really fall. The two continued to talk and the rest was history until one week later.

Natalia and Dumane planned to meet in Wilson to get away. She texted him and told him she had arrived at the hotel and that her phone would be dead. She checked into the hotel room, charged her phone to cut it back on. In came several text messages from dumane.

"Baby"

"Hello"

"Are you really ignoring me?"

"I'm driving to come see you and you don't want to text back"

"I'm getting ready to pull the fuck over"

"Baby please answer me: I love you, I know we just met"

"You're really done with me this fast?"

Natalia replied, "calm down, I'm at the hotel, I texted told you that my phone was going to die"

Thirty minutes passed and Natalia still didn't get a reply. She texted dumane and said "Hey, are you still coming?" She still got no reply.

Hysterical, she called her best friend Maria: "Girl, I traveled all the way to Wilson and he not answering my text, I've already paid for a hotel and if he doesn't show I'm going to be so upset." Maria said "give him time he might just be held up by traffic or might be pulling up now." Natalia said okay and hung up the phone. She looked out the hotel room, saw a grey Ferrari pull up and screamed in excitement.

The fact that this man just told her he loved her after a week, slipped her mind. She went outside in tears, he stepped out the car and apologized. "Baby, I'm so sorry. I was drinking with my brother, and then drove to you. I drunk Hennessey on the way driving to you which made me get sleepy and so I pulled over and took a nap." She forgave him and they went in the hotel room together. Sex was heavy on her mind as her pants began to be un-wearable. The only thing on Dumane's mind was how messed up his stomach was from drinking all that alcohol. He went to the bathroom with a cup full of more Hennessey and Dulce, pooping and drinking more alcohol.

After Dumane got out the restroom, the two slow kissed, then ran to the bed and had sex. Natalia ignored the fact that his penis had a lean to it because she really liked him. A dark moment filled with passionate kissing, Dumane trailed his tongue down to mouth her genitals. This provided a distraction from the fact he was slowly removing the condom, before sticking it back in, without her knowledge.

CHAPTER TWO:
FALLING FOR FIRE

The two woke up and he ran to his car to fill up another cup of coke, Hennessey, and Dulce. Walking back into the hotel quietly, attempting to not wake Natalia up; Dumane shuts the door and turns around to a beautiful Natalia sitting up staring straight at him. She asked "What's in the cup Dumane?" Dumane gave a straight face and replied "Breakfast."

Natalia looked in disbelief about his answer. She definitely didn't want no drunk, who couldn't piss without a swish of Hennessey telling him where to aim. Natalia asked him why he drank so much; Dumane shrugged with a guilty face and said that conversation is to be had at another time. Natalia ignored because she didn't want any more problems. Packing up and leaving the hotel the two gave each other a hug and kiss.

They both had gone back to their own cities. Natalia got home around 10am she texted dumane and like before no reply. Night time rolled in and still no text or call from dumane; she started to worry. "Are you okay?" "I'm really starting to worry about you dumane, please answer me." Natalia still did not receive a reply. The time now twelve midnight, Natalia started watching Netflix and fell asleep. 9:46am in the morning Natalia woke up to a phone call from dumane from a different number. She was excited to hear from him but at the same time upset because she had heard nothing from him in a whole day.

"Dumane. What happened?"

Dumane explained to her that he owns a business in Washington D.C and was also working on opening a business in charlotte which requires much of his time. He went on and stated that one of his main phones had messed up, so he had no choice but to put it in the shop. Natalia forgave him but asked why he changed his number? "I changed my number because I love you more than life and I'm serious about us, not these hoes". Dumane said without hesitation, almost like it was rehearsed. Natalia thought that was so sweet of him to say. After the two got off the phone: she texted him hey, but after three or four hours, she received no reply. A couple of days went buy and she hadn't heard anything. Finally, on the fifth day she got a response that read "hey baby I miss you". Distraught, but a little excited she called. No answer. At 9:46am he finally called back and said "Good morning love how are?"

"You know I called you right?"

He replied; "No, I never got any of your calls and I've been texting you for the last three days; have you been ignoring me? I really care about you and you promised me no drama with your ex and these last few days what the fuck have you been doing?"

"First of all, I've been texting and calling you, but you call at the same time every other day. I don't think I am going to be able to do this; we barley talk, do you live another life?" Natalia responded. The phone had become silent and after a while he managed to sweet talk her back into his charm because he knew he messed up, needed her money, her beauty, and her security.

Saturday came along and Natalia got a call from her mother around ten am about going to the fair. Natalia got dressed, got in her pretty blue bimmer, and headed down the highway. Getting off the exit towards her mother's house, Natalia gets a phone call from dumane. Excited she picked up the phone and said "hello babe, how are you?" Dumane quickly answered "love, where are you, I wanted to surprise you by stopping by but you're not home?" Natalia screamed at him "you came by my house and didn't tell me, you should've called me and told me I would've told my mom I'll meet up with her later." Dumane responded in a calm voice "it's okay babe, we can go somewhere later unless you want to meet up and go somewhere now." Without any hesitation Natalia canceled every plan and got back on the beltline. Natalia called dumane, he told her follow him up the road because he has a surprise for her.

Following blindly, Natalia agreed. Thirty minutes passed and Natalia realized she was out of her city. Out of curiosity she called dumane and asked him where are we going? Dumane kept playing it off by telling her we are almost there. Natalia's check oil light came on which caused her to have to pull over. She called dumane again and asked him, what's the destination? Natalia knew her car wasn't built for a long drive, but she also never really gotten out of her city other than when she goes home to Louisiana to visit family; so she didn't mind it.

She figured since her ex was so happy with the girl he had cheated on her with after 5 years, she needed to get out and have fun, be free, and just live by the yolo theme. Deep inside Natalia just wanted to be happy. Natalia spent most of her life caring and loving others more than herself. She enjoyed helping people which is why she was a teen ambassador for the three years she was in high school. Natalia had been homeless, had a boyfriend who stalked her and tried to kill her, and a lot of other unfortunate events. She still smiled and fought through everything, which is why she continued to drive down the highway blindly, hoping and wishing for a happy surprise at the end. Four hours passed and they finally reached a hotel around 330 in the afternoon. Natalia had no idea where she was. She and Dumane talked before he had to go to some business meeting; he told Natalia that he is going to take her out on the town; he wanted to buy her outfit, her food, her drinks, her shoes and give her the most incredible night she deserved.

CHAPTER THREE:
THE THRILL

Natalia was excited because her and her ex never went out on dates. She thought maybe, just maybe dates are a thing. Natalia kissed Dumane bye as he left the hotel to go to his business meeting. While lying in the hotel, Natalia started thinking what if I came up here for nothing, but she quickly erased it off her mind. She did not think a guy could be so full of shit. Six o'clock rolled around and she decided to run up the street to Walmart. She bought a cute outfit, a curling iron, feminine hygiene products and headed back to the hotel. Natalia jumped in the shower, got dressed and waited for his arrival.

Ten o'clock rolled around and she still hadn't heard anything. She agreed to wait till 11pm and if still no response, call everything off. Natalia laying down in disbelief looking straight up at the ceiling; it was 11:05pm. Natalia sent Dumane a text, "I'm all the way in another city for you, and you do this shit. I'm in shock and disbelief that you will do this. I'm getting ready to take a nap then I'm getting back on the road at 3am. Don't bother, I'm through. Natalia sent the text, then headed to taco bell to grab a bite to eat and went back to the hotel room.

Natalia ate her food in utter silence while watching family guy in her dark hotel room. Natalia could hear loud, ghetto shenanigan's next door to her hotel room. "Man, I was screwing this one girl and she was feeling so good and my girl walked in. I could not stop it was so wet: My girl was saying really Bryan, you going to just keep having sex with her in front of me? I told my girl I'm so sorry it was calling I couldn't stop. The next thing I know I felt hot water on my back, and I jumped up like I got shot in my ass."

Natalia stopped listening to the conversation, set an alarm for 330am, and went to sleep. Deep in her sleep at 316am, Natalia heard a loud knock on the door. She woke up and stared into the dark as if she couldn't fathom what was happening. The knock on the door got louder. She got up out of bed, and answered the door. To her surprise, dumane stood at the door looking guilty with glassy fish eye balls, a black du rag and black jacket. In his hands was a black trash bag and next to his beat up polo boots.

She looked at him and asked what do you want? He said "I know you're mad at me." Before finishing his sentence Natalia could smell the Hennessey and chitterling smell on his breath. She asked him had he been drinking and he stuttered "baby, I know your mad at me, I have been drinking just a little, I'm sorry I'm a busy man, I'm a business man and I was crunching numbers, drinking and I fell asleep. Can you please let me in?" Natalia looked in total disgust, but she let him in and the two went to bed. Natalia started to doze back off when Dumane turned over, grabbed her and said "baby I'm really hungry, can we go get something to eat?" She shrugged yes, got up, got dressed and headed out into the cold, and got into his Mercedes. The two went to cook out, he ordered his food and she a little something but nothing much. Natalia got out her card to pay for her portion of the meal and he said no, I can take care of it. The two got back to the hotel, ate, talked and layed down.

Dumane cuddled her as she dozed off. Natalia was half sleep when she felt him fully erect on the back of her butt. She fought and pleaded with herself. Don't you do it dam it!!!! Don't you do it. Natalia you are better than that. She eventually fought it off until Dumane's hands started to travel into her panties. Dumane felt how wet she was, sat up and said "I know you are not sleep, not as wet as you are." Natalia tried to ignore him as his lips softly started to kiss her neck, shoulders, and down her back. The night ended and the two woke up bright and early. Dumane woke up, filled a cup of Hennessey, sat on the toilet, drunk his breakfast and took a shower.

He told Natalia he had another business meeting to go to and he'd be back at eleven. She told him okay. Once he left Natalia started to pack up and leave soon after he left. It was 830 in the morning when he said he would be back at 11am. Now 1030 in the morning, Natalia walked out the door and got in her car to leave. She didn't care that he said he would be back at eleven. She was over his crap from last night.

Natalia started her car and then dumane walked up to the door and said "your just gonna leave me dam it." Natalia, stunned, said "no I was just warming my car", when in actuality she was leaving. The two got into their separate cars and headed down the highway. Natalia agreed to follow dumane because she didn't know where to go.

CHAPTER FOUR:
CLIMAXED

An hour into the drive dumane sped up and exited too fast for her to follow she called and asked him what he was doing. He said "oh I'm sorry just get off at the next exit and I'll tell you when to drive. Natalia pissed listened because she needed to know how to get home. The two finally got back onto the highway and drove for another hour. Dumane made a pit stop. Natalia thought he was going to gas station until she saw the liquor store on the right. Dumane pulled up to the liquor store got out and looked at Natalia in guilt.

Natalia put on her GPS and drove off. She was tired of his continuous drinking. She got home around 3pm, took a shower and laid down. Around 7pm she woke up to a knock on her door. She opened the door to a half intoxicated dumane. He barged into the house, kissed her and started to perform oral sex on her. She enjoyed it for some time but told him to stop because she was tired of his shit. He got up and the two started to talk. She explained to him her frustration and that her car was having serious problems now. She also explained her frustrations about his unreliability, his drinking, and his double life.

He apologized and agreed to work on it. The next day after class Natalia got a call from dumane. "Hey babe, I got a surprise for you: you said you were having car problems so I bought you a car. I need you to go to your bank and take out three thousand to give me on it and I can cover the rest." Natalia surprised and dumb went to the bank a pulled out the three thousand. Later that night he came over and collected the money and told her he was headed to go pick it up. The next morning she heard nothing. She started to get worried because she had already invested three hundred dollars into his business, and paid two hundred fifty nine dollars for his credit card bill because he lost his wallet. Natalia paced the floor beating her-self up repeating,

"How can I be so stupid?"

"This man needed somebody to live off of."

Natalia heard her phone ring. She rushed to her phone and it was dumane calling. She answered the phone and said "where is the car?" "Relax, He said softly you know I'm not that type of guy to lie, and steal from you." Natalia took a deep breath. He continued to tell her he had stuff to do this weekend, he'd be over the house the weekend to pick her up and take her to the car. Natalia exclaimed in happiness as the weekend was close by. Saturday came and Natalia had just gotten off work. Her job required her to get a flu shot to prepare for the upcoming season of the flu. This happened to be the same weekend of famous GHOE celebration. After her flu shot, she drove home and went to sleep. Natalia woke up five hours later to a dry gag, outrageous headache, and body that could barely move. She ignored as she tried to go to work. She had tried all day to get Dumane and tell him what was going on. No answer. She texted dumane from a co-workers phone to let him know that she was going to get checked out in ED and will be going home. Natalia knew he always complained that he never got her text, so she hoped that texting from another coworker's phone; he'd receive it and know what is going on.

Natalia co-worker, Angela said that she had received a text back. The text read,

"Where are you?"

"I came to the hospital they said they have no records of you at all?"

Natalia lost for words because she knew he was lying, so she went home and layed down. She texted him to tell him she was home safe and that she'd be fine. He texted her back at 200 in the morning saying he will be over. Natalia fell asleep and 345 in the morning dumane appeared at the door.

She asked him why it took him one hour and forty five minutes to get from his location to her if he was already here. He said traffic was bad. She knew he was lying because if he had just come from the hospital, it would've taken him twenty minutes and on top of that the celebration was one hour and thirty minutes away.

Natalia had one last question for him. She asked dumane what hospital he traveled to, to ask about her checking in. He stated that he went to a hospital on the opposite side of town and that the reception lady said she can check all hospitals systems, even hospitals that are not within the same company to see if I had checked in and/or being seen.

Natalia had enough at this point because this man was a habitual liar. She layed over and went to sleep until the sunrise woke the two of them up. Natalia got up and saw dumane walking around sore. Natalia asked him why was he so sore. Dumane answered "All that jumping and stomping around in GHOE." She said I thought you said you were in traffic and that you weren't going, he just smiled but didn't realize Natalia was through.

He told her he needed to have a serious talk with her.

CHAPTER FIVE: ALL HELL BREAKS LOOSE

Dumane brought Natalia down stairs to talk. Dumane said "I really love you more than life itself. I need to be honest with you. My business I own isn't all the way legal. I'm kind of in a mafia and they said if I pay one million dollars I'll be able to get out. I'll need to stay with you for several months and lay low.

Natalia took in the information as her heart began to drop. She had bad feelings about the guy when she first met him but she ignored it all for love, and to get over an ex. In that moment she knew there was no car, there was no business, and lastly that this man's life had deeper issues that she didn't want to find out about. She told him she was done with him and that she wanted her money back. He said what about the baby. Natalia screamed "what the fuck are you talking about?"

He told her what he did and that if there was a baby, he will have all his lawyers take it away from her. He proceeded to call her a stupid bitch and walk off. Natalia mad, scared, and lost for words tried to think when her last period was. As she thought long and hard she remembered it wasn't due yet.

Natalia laid down and watched Netflix, crying herself to sleep because she finally came to her census. Natalia was a very smart girl but she let her vulnerability get the best of her. Natalia owned a house, a car, a business in addition to working for an excellent company at a young age. She cried because she almost lost all of it not being smart.

Natalia went and came clean to her dad about everything. He said chuck it up as a loss and move in. She was mad because she had several car problems and couldn't get a new car because all the money she shelled out, plus the loan she took out. Her dad told her God will see you through this just trust him and that everyone comes into your life for a reason. You might not see the reason now but I can see you are back thinking how you are supposed to, you are over your ex, and your back on your grind that got you as far as you did today.

Even though Natalia couldn't stop beating her-self up, she listened. With the help of her Co-workers and business partners she started to get back happy even though she was struggling still. Weeks passed by and she had heard nothing from Dumane. Natalia woke up one morning and decided to look at her bank account. She found a message stating a NSF charge was completed on her checking account. She opened it and to her surprise a check was made out to a Dumane Jones for eighteen hundred dollars. Natalia screamed because she never wrote that check. She ran to place she kept her check book because it was also where she kept her spare key and just like she thought, the spare key and one check was missing.

Natalia rushed to the bank with her father on the phone. She demanded to speak with somebody. She explained the situation to him. The teller said to her "You need to walk out of here and call the cops and get a restraining order. You need to do whatever it is you need to do to keep yourself safe. No man should have you scared to live." Natalia took his advice and sought legal action but they were very limited on what they can do. They couldn't give her a restraining order because they needed proof. She knew dumane would never text her nothing stupid to incriminate his self. Instead he would drive around the neighborhood at night. A couple of weeks later; Natalia had a friend over and they chilled and watched Netflix.

Natalia's friend stood up and said somebody is outside. Her gut dropped to her stomach because she low-key knew that dumane was outside her door. She stood up and seen a six three figure outside her window staring back at them. Natalia froze but her friend said I'm going outside and I'm going to f him up something nice. Before her friend can get outside he took off running to his car.

CHAPTER SIX: FINISHED

Natalia woke up in the morning to find both her and her friend fell asleep. She woke him up and told him to leave because he had to be to work and he was already late. She gave him a hug and he walked off. As Natalia turned around, a long furry tail caught her eye. She looked closely at the object until she realized it was a perfectly skinned squirrel with the tail still in tack. She panicked and called the cops again.

The cops explained that until you actual get a visual threat, they can't do anything. Natalia lost for words decided to send one final text to him. "Dumane, I know how you stole a check and tried to cash it, you can get major jail time for what you did. I know all about you. You are a fraud and I can end it all right now for you. You keep the fucking money; just leave me the fuck alone. Just know God will handle you accordingly."

Natalia knew that this was very risky but at this point she wanted to try one last thing. A couple of weeks passed by and weeks turned into months and she heard nothing. Maybe he died in car wreck or went to jail, Natalia didn't know but she didn't care neither because he left her alone. Natalia started picking up the pieces that were hammered off and putting it back where it belonged. Although it would still take her a while to go back to where she was mentally, emotionally, physically, and financially one thing was for sure, she was over her ex and she grew more spiritually.

Natalia learned that sometimes when God removes somebody out of your life it is for your good. It is never good to go look-ing for a replacement or Space filler because you will get some-thing you never wished for. Natalia learned that it is okay to be vulnerable because it teaches you how to love and be peaceful in your own company. It might hurt for a little while and you might feel very alone but you will always come out on top, you just have to keep pushing through it. Do not rejoice in others karmas, stay humble, stay true and remember;

Love thy self before anyone else.

ABOUT THE AUTHOR

J D Whitaker

Based on a True Story, J D, who goes by jo, Was born August 9, and loves writing. Jo, attended high school in North Carolina where she skipped 11th grade. She then went on to graduate college three times, earning her three degree's. She enjoys being a Nurse. She was a Teen ambassador for NC and State Finalist for North Carolina's National American Miss Pageant.

She now dually owns Life Line Care LLC, educating people on how to perform CPR and National Distrubution of AED.

She also enjoys planning health events.

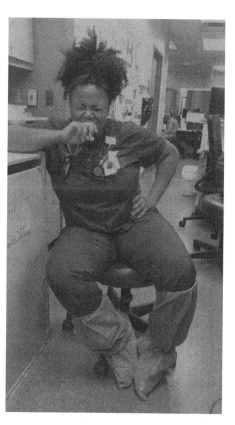

Follow her on instagram _Powerhousejo

Follow her Author Page on Amazon J D Whitaker

BOOKS BY THIS AUTHOR

Without A Fight - Fight To Finish

Second part to Without A Fight is coming soon. Stayed Tuned.

Tornatic Depression

Book of poetry for the soul. Coming soon. To submit your poetry for a chance to be included, follow the author on instagram to stay up on how to enter.
10 People will be selected.

Made in the USA
Columbia, SC
03 February 2022

55346715R00017